THE ~A~ BRIDGE

Prophet Brandon L
The ~A~ Bridge

Published by Spines
ISBN: 979-8-89569-210-3

THE ~A~ BRIDGE

HELLS RUMOR

PROPHET BRANDON L

CONTENTS

PREFACE

I thank my God through Jesus Christ for you all. Your faith is spoken of throughout the whole world. For God is my witness, whom I serve in the gospel of His Son, that without ceasing I make mention of you always in my prayers. I desire to impart unto you knowledge, wisdom, understanding, and some spiritual gift, that you may be established and understand that the word of God is real. It's quick, it's powerful—more powerful than any two-edged sword, dividing asunder the soul and the spirit, and is a discerner of the thoughts and intents of the heart.

People, saints, and sinners hesitate when it comes to reading material that talks about Hell. Everyone wants to hear about Heaven, and the funny thing is most people think that after they die, they're going to Heaven.

The sad thing is, not everyone will make it. The truth of the matter is, everyone can perceive you as a good person by your name and many accomplishments, but if you have not received Jesus Christ and the work that He did on Calvary, you cannot inherit the kingdom of God.

It's funny—it took so long for me to finish this book. I did part of it with audio and part of it by typing with speech-to-text, so there's also going to be an audio version of the book, along with the ebook, which will be available for download online. Now, all of us believe that our writings are very important, and especially in the Christian community, we want everyone to tap into what God has shown us. It's so crazy—when using this audio text, every time I mention God, it puts a lowercase "g," and we know that's not right, but the devil is a liar. I'm here to talk to you about the grace, mercy, power, and presence of God, and how we should seek that power and presence every moment of our lives.

We cannot take a chance on our ability to do anything, especially when it comes to going to Heaven. The Bible tells us in John 3:16: For God so loved the world, that He gave His only begotten Son, that whoever believes in Him shall not perish but have everlasting life. So that means that God knew we would fall short, He knew we would be on our way to Hell, so He made a sacrifice—He gave up His only begotten Son to stand in the gap for us, because the wages of sin is death, but the gift of God is eternal life through Jesus Christ our Lord.

So, I had to ask myself the question: why write this book when most people who read it will not believe the accounts in it? No one wants to hear about Hell, and many people don't believe that Hell exists. And because of that widespread belief here on Earth, people think they can just live the way they want, and when it's all said and done, they'll see their family again in Heaven.

I came to try and shake things up and put in order some beliefs about Heaven and Hell here on Earth. This is a very serious subject, and it will lock you into a state of curiosity. For the next couple of hours, I want you to forget everything you know and have heard about death and what happens to us after we die. Lose yourself in these pages and ask yourself, "What if?" And if you are an atheist or a skeptic, take a walk with us into a story entitled *The ~A~ Bridge*.

This book is an actual description of an event that took place almost five years ago—an out-of-body experience and transport to a place called Hell. God desires for every soul to at least have the opportunity to be saved. Prayerfully, my vision, dream, and experience will prompt you to take a closer look at your life, your attitude, and the way you treat people, especially the way you treat God.

INTRODUCTION

There is a weird feeling in the air, a sort of evil spirit lurking around every corner. I could not figure out why it took so long to finish this book, but now I see that the release is all about God's timing. He wanted to make sure that every detail was addressed and expressed, that which is necessary for the advancement of His people.

It is a powerful day when you find yourself in the will of God. Even just the conversation that can transpire between you and God. Of course, there are some days when we can't even hear our own voice, follow instructions, or complete a task. When you have those days and experiences, you must remember that you can do all things through Christ who strengthens you.

It's truly amazing when we have these strange encounters, visions, and dreams—some of which are very odd and may be due to needing rest or a change in diet. And then there are times when you dream something that you know holds significant meaning.

Now, concerning this particular book, unlike others that took almost four years to finish, I had to be sure I didn't leave out any important details nor add my own. This subject is a big reason why many people don't believe what we believe as Christians: people just don't believe there is a Hell.

Therefore, they see no reason to fear God and obey Him because, according to many who preach inclusion, God is going to forgive everyone, whether they repent or not. That mentality or theory kept me up many nights, just shaking my head. We have become so complacent, arrogant, and disobedient that the word of God is no longer respected and honored as God's voice today.

We are in the last days—people are protecting what is wrong and shunning what is right. It is becoming dangerous in the United States to stand up for your belief in God, and don't you dare mention Jesus. In fact, the scriptures say in John 10:27-30: *My sheep hear My voice, and I know them, and they follow Me: 28 And I give unto them eternal life, and they shall never perish, neither shall any man pluck them out of My hand. 29 My Father, which gave them to Me, is greater than all; and no man can pluck them out of My Father's hand. 30 I and My Father are one.*

So if you are of the group that thinks Jesus was just a prophet, think again. Jesus is God in the flesh. He came to pay a sin debt that He didn't owe. Therefore, if any man is in Christ, he is a new creature. Old things have passed away, and behold, all things have become new. All have sinned and come short of His glory—White, Black, Yellow, Man, Woman—all have come short and have missed the mark. What mark? Obedience, staying in His will, and being in the right relationship with Him. Outside of that, there is punishment. Just like here on Earth, if you break the law, there are consequences for each crime. The same is true in the kingdom of God. If you choose not to believe in Him and receive His Son as your Savior and Lord, there are consequences. Those who are the children of God, who were born again and received Jesus Christ as Lord and Savior, will spend eternity in Heaven with God. Those who have chosen to mock Him and transgress His law will be punished. God is not a man that He should lie.

So in saying that, this story, though troubling, is very powerful and should take all of its readers on a ride they will never forget: *The ~A~ Bridge.* The ~A~ Bridge is a place in Hell where the people who are there believe that they can return to their lives and have another chance after death.

PART I

A GLIMPSE INTO THE ABYSS

MIND GAMES

We often sit in many places and begin to think back or reminisce about the past. Oftentimes, we find ourselves daydreaming about a particular person, place, or thing. It captivates us, and many times we don't know why we are there or what causes our minds to drift off. Some of us are thinkers, meaning we often try to solve problems for another time or day, no matter where we are. What about you? Are you one who remembers your dreams? Many nights, you have had crazy dreams and remembered every detail, but there are other times when we can only remember small details that usually don't make any sense.

I want to suggest to you not to ignore anything that you dream about because there could be a hidden message somewhere in those details. It could be obvious, or it could be a message from God. How about those of you who have dreams about events or situations, sometimes dangerous situations like accidents, etc., and later on, you find out that the dream actually came true?

Sometimes the Devil wants to mess with your mind and get you off track and out of focus so that you will be distracted from what God is trying to tell you to do. The devil comes to steal, kill, and destroy, so it would be a good idea to pay attention and take heed of your surroundings and the people you associate with. Your mind is very powerful, and the great thing about God is He trusts you to make the right decisions and to feed your mind with the right stuff, the right information, and knowledge. I believe all of this has a lot to do with what you dream about.

For instance, I watched a scary movie once, and when I went to bed, I had to leave the lights on because I was scared. How about I had a nightmare about the movie that I had just watched? There was nothing prophetic about the dream. It was just something that frightened me.

Many times, we have the wrong stuff on our minds when we go to bed. That's why the Lord tells us that man ought always to pray, and that we should pray without ceasing. Many times, there are situations that we come across in life or even something that we have caused ourselves. And it comes from us not feeding our minds with the right information.

Sin is a big problem, especially in these last and evil days. You have to ask God to renew your mind daily. Your mind is a battlefield, and the kingdom of darkness wants to control your mind with evil thoughts, bad decisions, cursing, swearing, and arguing being at the forefront. He wants you to forfeit the blessing that God has prepared for you from the foundation of the world. The Bible says that Jesus came that we might have life and life more abundantly. The Lord is our Shepherd, and we shall not want. And when we do want and need and fall short, He restores our soul.

Most of the time, our problem has nothing to do with what someone said or did to us, but what is going on between our ears and the thoughts that oftentimes cause us to sin against God.

The book of Romans says in [Rom 12:1-2]:

1: I beseech you therefore, brethren, by the mercies of God, that ye present your bodies a living sacrifice, holy, acceptable unto God, [which is] your reasonable service.

2: And be not conformed to this world: but be ye transformed by the renewing of your mind, that ye may prove what [is] that good, and acceptable, and perfect, will of God.

And along with that, we must remember that:

[Rom 8:1 KJV]

1: [There is] therefore now no condemnation to them which are in Christ Jesus, who walk not after the flesh, but after the Spirit.

So it is very important to pray unto God so you can know the will of God for your life. You must be born again. Once you are born again, you will begin to study the word with a greater understanding and secure your victory with what Jesus did for us on Calvary and the fact that God raised Him up on the third day morning with all power in His hands.

Now, believe it or not, there are many people out there that don't want you to be saved and, most of all, do not want you to know the truth. There are many false prophets out there, but there are also true prophets of God that He is uncovering in these last days to prophesy and to forthtell events that are soon to come. Set your affections on things that are above and cast your care on Him, for He cares for you. Do not let the enemy play mind games with you and have you believing the lies of Satan. Jesus is the Christ, the Son of the living God.

2

PROPHETIC DREAMS AND VISIONS

It has really been a challenge to stay focused on the task at hand. How many times do we try to accomplish something for God, to try to do the work for the kingdom, and it seems like every step, at every corner, there is a problem, predicament, or situation that tries to interfere and distract you? But I came to encourage you today and let you know that you will finish strong if you keep your focus on God.

This chapter is leading to an important part of this book, dealing with prophetic dreams and visions. Many of us that I talk to ignore our dreams based on subject matter. I come to tell you to start documenting them because we are in the last days, and God may use you and your dream or vision to bring forth a message. Because during the last days, any part of the day that may save someone's life, bring someone to Christ, or set someone free and deliver them from the attacks that have consumed their life, that is a good day. God said, "And my daughter shall prophesy."

INTRODUCTION

There is a weird feeling in the air, a sort of evil spirit lurking around every corner. I could not figure out why it took so long to finish this book. But now I see that the release is all about the timing of God. He wanted to make sure that every detail was addressed and expressed—that which is necessary for the advancement of His people.

It is a powerful day when you find yourself in the will of God for most of the day. Even just the conversation that can transpire between you and God. Now, of course, there are some days when we can't even hear our own voice, nor follow instructions, or complete a task. When you have those days and experiences, you have to remember that you can do all things through Christ who strengthens you.

It's truly amazing that at times we have these strange encounters, strange visions, and dreams. Some of which are very dull and due to needing to catch up on your rest or change your diet. And then there are times when you dream something that you know has significant meaning.

Now, concerning this particular book—unlike others, this took almost 4 years to finish. I just had to be sure I didn't leave out any important details, nor add my own. This subject is a big reason a lot of people don't believe what you believe as a Christian. People just don't believe there is a Hell.

Therefore, there is no reason to fear God and obey Him because, according to many who preach inclusion, God is going to forgive everyone whether they repent or not. That mentality or theory had me up many nights, just shaking my head. We have gotten so complacent, arrogant, and disobedient that the Word of God is not respected and honored as God's voice today.

We are in the last days. People are protecting what is wrong and shunning what is right. It is becoming dangerous in the United States to stand up for your belief in God, and don't you dare mention Jesus. When, in fact, the scriptures say in John 10:27-30:

"My sheep hear my voice, and I know them, and they follow me:

28. And I give unto them eternal life; and they shall

never perish, neither shall any man pluck them out of my hand.

29. My Father, which gave them me, is greater than all; and no man is able to pluck them out of my Father's hand.

30. I and my Father are one."

So if you are of the group that believes Jesus was just a prophet, think again. Jesus is God in the flesh. He came to pay a sin debt that He didn't owe. "Therefore, if any man be in Christ, he is a new creature. Old things are passed away, and behold, all things have become new." All of us have sinned and come short of His glory. White, Black, Yellow, Man, Woman, all have come short and have missed the mark. What mark?

Obedience, staying in His will, and being in right relationship with Him. Outside of that, there is punishment, just like here on earth—if you break the law, there are consequences for each crime. The same is true in the Kingdom of God. If you choose not to believe in Him and receive His Son as your Savior and Lord, there are consequences. Those who are the children of God, who were born again, who received Jesus Christ as Lord and Savior, will spend eternity in Heaven with God. Those who have chosen to mock Him and transgress His law will be punished.

God is not a man that He should lie. So, in saying

that, this story, though troubling, is very powerful and should take all of its readers on a ride they will never forget: "The ~A~ Bridge." The ~A~ Bridge is a place in Hell where the people who are there believe that they can return to their lives and have another chance after dying.

3

CHAOS AND DISORDER

Looking at the news will depress you and really put you in a negative mindset if you don't reflect on what God says about these last and evil days. He said there would come scoffers walking after their own lusts, saying, "Where is the promise of His coming?"

He said there would be perilous times. With every shooting—black on black, white on black, and police killing young black men—I shake my head and say, "Lord, how long?" God always reminds me that while on this earth, we have free moral agency, which means we had a choice. Some choose to do good, and most choose to do bad, and live life not according to any purpose or plan, but how to get that money.

It's crazy. I was driving down the street toward home, and a dirt bike went flying through the traffic, weaving and bobbing in and out between the cars. Then behind him were about 50 other motorcycles, scooters, and ATVs popping wheelies and driving on both sides of the street. They took over the neighborhoods. I know that during these times, especially when our youth rebel, Satan has a good time because his work is being done on a high scale. It's hard to pray for your enemies during these times, but God commands us to do it. Not only that, but we have to bless those who curse us and despitefully use us. I know you say, "Wow," and shake your head, but it's the only way to save people from a fiery, burning Hell for all of eternity.

It is becoming like it was during the time of Noah. God had repented that He made man. And if you remember, eventually, there came consequences for their actions. There was chaos and disorder in the time of Lot. God gave him an opportunity to get out of the city because His wrath was coming. Fire rained down and destroyed Sodom and Gomorrah because of their lewdness and sexual immorality—men with men and women with women doing that which is unseemly or unnatural. Now, it's becoming almost illegal to preach the Gospel of Jesus Christ and witness to someone to persuade them to come to the Lord. Groups and protesters, who are being led by the devil, try to convince us that they were born this way. Now sexual preference is a civil right and is looked upon as the new black or the new "n-word."

Our children are being taught craziness about homosexuality as if it is some good thing—confusing our youth and turning the world upside down. Now, they feel it has to be incorporated into every TV show and movie.

The Bible says in [1Co 6:9 KJV], "Know ye not that the unrighteous shall not inherit the kingdom of God? Be not deceived: neither fornicators, nor idolaters, nor adulterers, nor effeminate, nor abusers of themselves with mankind."

    i. Effeminate defined: a boy kept for homosexual relations with a man.
    ii. A male who submits his body to unnatural lewdness.
    iii. A male prostitute.

So, this also pertains to women. God is not mocked. Whatever a man sows, that shall he also reap.

It has been shown to us who are of the faith that we need to step up our game. Many of us have so much trouble going on in our own lives that we find it hard to be involved or to participate in evangelizing the lost. But I say unto you that we must share the gospel, or even some of our family members might perish. Going to Hell is a real thing, not just a story in a book.

Let's focus on the chaos and disorder and zero in our prayers to stop some of this chaos even before it happens. God gave us prayer for that purpose. We have to have a preventive mindset. We can't stop and diminish the strength of evil and of the Devil. God tells us to resist him, and he shall flee from us. We have the blood of the Lamb and the word of our testimony to help us overcome and be victorious.

Funny that we never hear of any testimonies of those who have been delivered from homosexuality. Why? Many are afraid of what those who are in that lifestyle would think of them. So, right now, in the name of Jesus, I decree and declare that we will see more testimonies of divine deliverance from lesbianism and homosexuality.

Knowing that there are many things going on around us and in the background, prejudice and racism still exist on a high level worldwide. Even in the church, we are still the white church, the black church, or the Latino church. I really believe Jesus is soon to come, and we will have to answer for all of the dysfunction in our homes, workplaces, and the church. The more I think on these things, I cry out to God and say, "Lord, show us Your power. Help us to defeat this enemy." People are dying daily from opioid overdoses and other addictions, and they are all affecting our children.

Every conversation, illustration, and description above reflects the things that we do that affect people, families, children, and most of all, the word of God. So, as I go back through these thoughts, processing these things and the problems of life, I wonder why I went to Hell first. I am a Christian and believe that Jesus Christ was raised from the dead on the third day, and that repentance and remission of sins should be preached in His name. I believe Jesus Christ rose from the dead on the third day with all power in His hands.

Then, one day in my room on the second floor, I was sitting on the edge of my bed. I can't remember if the TV was on or off, but the next thing I know, my chest was hurting, and I left my body. It was like I was floating in the air above my body. I could see myself slouched over on the bed in a sitting position, so my first thoughts were that I had died. I didn't know if I was dreaming or whether this was a vision or nightmare. All I know is I was looking at myself, and I was not breathing. There was no movement nor reaction. I was gone.

Now, according to what I believe to be the truth, when a Christian dies, or when one dies who has faith in Jesus Christ, they are considered a child of God, and after death, we live in eternity. Yes, go ahead and say it,

"Jesus Christ." Those who disobey His Word do not believe He is who He says He is (atheists), and those that worked evil on this Earth, controlled by Satan, will ultimately end up in hell.

But this did not happen for me; that is the scary part. After I saw myself on the bed, I was transported to a place that looked like I was at the top of a mountain or at a cliff. When I looked down, there was nothing but smoke, terrible smells, and fire as far as I could see. While I was standing there, I felt a presence next to me, and then before I knew it, they pushed me off the cliff. I began falling so far, but I was falling slowly.

The next thing I knew, I hit the ground, but I wasn't injured. It was almost like when I got close to the bottom, I slowed down even more to avoid injury.

So, I'm telling you I went to Hell, but I didn't go as a resident. I went as a spectator, an observer. It was crazy. There were people everywhere screaming and cursing. Some were chained, some were men, women, executives, some teenagers, policemen, sheriffs, agents, politicians, TV personalities, athletes, superstars, billionaires, educators, pretty, handsome, and those considered to be great here on Earth were now in hell.

The thing that was so unique about this experience, whether it be a dream, vision, or an actual out-of-body experience, is that everywhere I went, there was a rumor

—different rumors, different lies continuously—and it was hot above my head with smoke, maybe six or seven feet above my head. There was fire, and the fire and smoke were constantly rolling, like we have the sky on Earth. The sky for them is fire, so it was almost like the feeling of an iron or the feeling of when you get burned by grease, but it never stops and it's increased almost ten times worse than it is on Earth.

I'm in hell. I'm walking around trying to figure out how to get out, and I could hear people talking about this rumor that if you can get to the ~A~ Bridge, you can get back to your life and leave hell once and for all. Now, there is no record of anyone going to hell and coming back, but Jesus Christ in the Bible says He went to hell to get the keys, to snatch the keys to the kingdom of Satan. Therefore, He conquered death, hell, and the grave and was risen on the third day by God from the dead. He conquered death and gave us victory, but I was not in that place of victory. I went to hell after I died.

This feeling I had was a feeling of sadness, and it seemed like I was crying continuously. I saw people I knew. They could not hear what I was saying to them, but I could hear them cursing me for not setting them straight, so I kept walking. I saw Gypsy people I had seen on TV, people who were in my college, people I went to high school with. It just seemed like everyone I thought would have gone to heaven found themselves in hell. It was hot, and I was sweating. There was continuous heat, and it was hard to breathe, hard to think, and I just kept going forward.

I wanted to see this place—hell's rumored ~A~ Bridge is far off, maybe about 1 or 2 miles. I could see something that was raised above the fire like a skyscraper, so I kept walking. People kept calling my name and grabbing my arm. The crowd was confused. Some places were full of mud, and other places were almost like a junkyard where you walk in and see cars stacked up. It felt like I was in a junkyard, but these were human beings, and it was terrifying. It was sad, but there was nothing I could do.

After a few hours, I finally ended up in this place where the grass was burned up, and there were people standing in lines, several rows. You could see people fighting for position. I saw a structure, so I went to this structure and looked up. I was transported above the smoke and fire. It was shaped like an "A," and it was a bridge. I believe the Lord sent me here to let people know that hell is real, that there is weeping and gnashing of teeth, there is constant pain, anguish, sadness, and it's terrible. The best word I could use for this is terrible.

I'm above the smoke and above the fire, and I'm just

floating. Then I'm transported to the top of this structure that literally looks like an "A"—the ~A~ Bridge. I got to the top of the area, and the top of the bridge was about 50 by 50, so it was a small area at the top of the bridge. I looked over the edge, and I saw this long line of people holding on to each other's ankles, feet, and waistlines. They were snatching each other from the human rope, and people were going back into the fire. Folks were rude to each other. They were cussing, fighting, believing they would get another chance to live their life.

I went around all sides of this area at the top of ~A~ Bridge, and there were people everywhere, hanging on the bridge, trying to climb up the sides to get to the top. Above the area where I stood, the sky was cloudy. It almost looked like the sky, but it was a gold color, and above that, I saw a cross. The rumor has it that if you get to ~A~ Bridge and reach the top, you can go back to your life on Earth and be forgiven.

The funny thing is, neither God nor Jesus is ever mentioned. The fact that they lived their lives the way they wanted to, never repented of their sins, and did not believe that Jesus Christ was the Son of God was never mentioned. Only the rumors went back and forth, back and forth. All of these people that were in hell—some were in suits that were burned, some were in dresses—

but all of their clothes were smoky and burned, and everybody looked beaten down and terribly wounded.

I was in tears. There was compassion in my heart, and I wanted to preach the gospel to them, but I could not preach. I was in hell, but I was a Christian, and I had to ask myself at the top of ~A~ Bridge, "Lord, why am I here? I believed in You. I trusted You. I repented of my sins, and I waited to live eternity with You, but I went to hell?"

The only thing I could think of to do was to try to help these people who were hanging off the edge of this bridge and try to pull them up to safety. Below them, there was fire everywhere, so I pulled out the first person. I'm so happy they went on the other side of the platform, which was only 50 x 50. Then I pulled up the next person and the next person.

People started snatching each other down off of this line. There was a line of people hanging off of the top of ~A~ Bridge, off of the metal bracket braces and the things that held the bridge together. They were hanging all around this area at the top of the bridge, which was 50 by 50, so more people were at the top with me, and I had them help me pull people up to the platform to safety.

But the problem is, I was in hell. There was no compassion, there was no love. There was only desperation and deception, so the people that were trying to help me, supposedly, were really pulling people up and throwing them back down into the fire. You see, we were running out of room. It was only 50 ft by 50 ft, and only a certain amount of people could exist up there. At the same time, some people were trying to snatch me down when I was trying to pull them up, and it was disappointing and frustrating.

I was trying to save these people, but their attitudes were jacked up. They were cursing me, spitting on me, and people were falling back into the fire. There were some young kids in hell. They were about 15 or 16 years old, and they were climbing on top of women, putting their feet on their shoulders and their heads. It was terrible.

I said, "I have to help these people get up and out of here," so I had to ask myself, "Do you really believe that they can climb to the top of this bridge, climb up to the sky and the cross, and be redeemed and set free to live their life as if they never died?"

This whole thing was so dramatic. I felt so out of place. I knew I shouldn't have been there. I knew I should have been in heaven, but I had no control and no power over my placement, and I couldn't remember the past. All I knew was, in my heart, I had Christ, and He was in me, and I was in Him, but I was in hell.

Then I felt the presence of why all these people were screaming and gnashing their teeth and falling back into the fire. I could hear a whisper in my ear saying, "You can't do that. You can't save them." I don't know if it was an angel, but it was God Himself. All I know is He said, "My son, this is the problem that I have with the church. The compassion is there, the drive is there, the determination is there, but you are trying to save people in your own power."

"And this is how the church has been functioning for hundreds of years: singing songs, preaching my gospel, helping my people, baptizing them in the name of the Father, and the Son, and the Holy Ghost. But there are some churches, some preachers, some pastors, some prophets, some evangelists that believe they have the power to pull people out of hell with their own power."

After this was said to me, I felt terrible. I was only trying to help, but what the voice told me was that this was the wrong way to help. The top of the ~A~ Bridge was full of people, and it was packed all the way to the edge on the east side, and no one knew what to do next. I looked up at the sky at the cross and was in tears because I couldn't help.

The next thing I knew, I was transported back to the cliff, miles and miles away from where I first saw a hill. I felt a presence beside me. I couldn't see who it was, but it felt like I was in the presence of God. He said, "Now let's go back, and I will show you." Then I knew that God was speaking to me, so I felt a push on my back, and I fell down again into this rolling smoke and fire. And the Lord told me he was going to walk with me and interpret what I'd seen. So while he was walking with me, I felt his presence, but I also felt death, sadness, weeping, and gnashing of teeth, people grabbing for us, cursing at us, crying out, and God began to interpret the situation, describing this out-of-body experience to me.

4

PESHAR: THE INTERPRETATION

There is a unique relationship between God and me. He allows me to dream prophetic dreams, many of which come to pass, and if I ask Him, He will return me to the dream. Sometimes, I can get up and go to the bathroom, get some water, go back and lay down, go back to sleep, and God will come in the dream and interpret the dream for me. He's done this several times.

Concerning the ~A~ Bridge, He takes me back to the beginning. I'm standing on a cliff, looking down at the smoke and the fire, which stretches for miles and miles. He tapped me on the back, and I fell off the cliff, down to the bottom, through the fire and smoke, and I'm back in Hell again. Except this time, instead of being terrified, instead of crying my eyes out, feeling this sense of weakness, I was able to control what was going on, where I was going, and how I was moving.

Now God was with me, and He walked me through the dream—not frantic or out of pace, nor with worry or fear. This time, walking through, I knew I wasn't an observer, and I could feel He trusted me to go back and warn people about this place. I began to think while we were walking: if there is a court system and supposedly justice here on Earth, why wouldn't there be justice in the kingdom of God? Some people go to jail for 20 and 30 years, committing murder and crimes of passion, and drug addiction. If there is a prison cell, why wouldn't there be a hell for those who don't believe in God?

We were walking, and He turned right. It was almost like we were on three streets, one on each side of us. Some people were bound, some were chained, some were in cages, but all were in prison and in Hell, separated from God. They're saying they had no Savior, so they thought, so they ignored God and His word, simple words from John 3:16: *"For God so loved the world that He gave His only begotten Son, that whosoever believes in Him shall not perish, but have everlasting life."* We walked and walked, and He wanted me to see the people that ended up in this place. He told us in the word that the gate is narrow, and that many will come to Him saying, "Lord, Lord," and He will say, *"I never knew you. Depart from me, you workers of iniquity."* While I was walking with Him, I could feel wisdom come over me; I could feel understanding come over me, and He began to let me reflect on what I've seen in this life and how people have taken the Gospel of Jesus Christ for granted.

We kept walking, and He touched me, and I could feel the power of God like never before. We turned left and kept walking. There were judges and lawyers, sheriffs deputies, singers, band members, songwriters, producers, directors, movie stars, race car drivers, teachers, and principals. Almost every walk of life had taken part in ignoring God, not receiving Jesus as Lord, and lifting up their eyes in Hell. We kept walking, and we turned left again and went down this aisle. Now, remember, I told you it was just like a junkyard—if you've ever been in a junkyard where there are cars stacked on cars, trucks, and SUVs. It seemed that people were put in certain areas by categories of what the sin was that so easily beset them. All the murderers were in the same area, all the thieves, all the liars, all the drug addicts, all the pedophiles, all the rapists, and all the adulterers were grouped together in this massive area. God reminded me of the story.

Luke 16:19-31 (New International Version)
The Rich Man and Lazarus
19 "There was a rich man who was dressed in purple

and fine linen and lived in luxury every day. 20 At his gate was laid a beggar named Lazarus, covered with sores 21 and longing to eat what fell from the rich man's table. Even the dogs came and licked his sores.

22 "The time came when the beggar died, and the angels carried him to Abraham's side. The rich man also died and was buried. 23 In Hades, where he was in torment, he looked up and saw Abraham far away, with Lazarus by his side. 24 So he called to him, 'Father Abraham, have pity on me and send Lazarus to dip the tip of his finger in water and cool my tongue, because I am in agony in this fire.'

25 "But Abraham replied, 'Son, remember that in your lifetime you received your good things, while Lazarus received bad things, but now he is comforted here, and you are in agony. 26 And besides all this, between us and you a great chasm has been set in place, so that those who want to go from here to you cannot, nor can anyone cross over from there to us.'

27 "He answered, 'Then I beg you, father, send Lazarus to my family, 28 for I have five brothers. Let him warn them, so that they will not also come to this place of torment.'

29 "Abraham replied, 'They have Moses and the Prophets; let them listen to them.'"

30 "'No, father Abraham,' he said, 'but if someone from the dead goes to them, they will repent.'

31 "He said to him, 'If they do not listen to Moses and the Prophets, they will not be convinced even if someone rises from the dead.'"

Their conversation and exchange were devastating and sad; it was true and needed for us to see that hell is real and that once you cross over, there is no coming back. The terrifying thing was, as I walked, people were screaming, fussing, and cursing, trying to get a loose summer chain. Many were in these lots; it seemed like all the people that had similar sayings were grouped together in this mud and sitting in sulfur and ashes, and your skin was burning constantly, like if you held an iron onto your arm or leg forever.

As I looked around, it seemed that every aisle I went down, there was somebody I knew—somebody from my family, somebody from school, somebody from college, someone from TV, television shows, people that gave to charity. I mean, it seemed like most of the people down there did good things in their life, but their hearts were not with God. So in the end, the end came, and people were looking and wondering which way they would go. They turned to Him, and the Lord said, "I never knew you. Depart from me, you workers of iniquity."

One thing you don't hear in hell is anyone preaching the gospel. It seems as if it was wiped from their minds, but now that they're separated from God, they can't even remember what they knew. All they remember is what they see. Now, I believe it's possible for them to remember their family because the rich man cried out to Abraham and told him to go back and warn his family about this place.

It's so sad. The youngest person I saw there was about 15, but I didn't see very many young people. Most of the people I saw were people that I recognized and knew, people I had crossed paths with in some situation, and some were people that I had witnessed to while evangelizing out on the streets. There were a few people whose names I could remember, but I could not tell them anything or speak to them. This was all thoughts in my mind. For some reason, I could not speak. I could hear people screaming, speaking, cursing, and like the Bible says, there was weeping and gnashing of teeth. Constant pain because of disobedience—so sad, but there was nothing I could do. It seemed like I had more than a half-mile to go to get to the place where every one of them was trying to get to, and still a bridge. So I kept going. God was leading me down these different houses, these different streets, these different areas, and I would see something different every time I went down. There was never anything pleasant on my way—so sad.

For instance, some areas I walked down, I would see a group of people, and I would see a whole bunch of things like a trailer to a movie. Sometimes in these little previews for trailers, I would see murders, robberies, abuse—family, children, adults, seniors in pain. Each area I walked past, sometimes it was just one person by themselves, and you would see their movie. I mean, whatever they did, the sin that so easily beset them, was playing while I was walking. In some places, I walked with groups of people in the mud and sulfur, crying and weeping. Some of them had no movie—it seemed like the screen was blank, and it was quiet, dark, and spooky. So I kept walking.

I was thinking about God. I was thankful that I knew Him and was freed from my sins. I began to reflect on when I was saved, but while I was walking, I was wondering, when I died, why didn't I go to heaven? Why did I end up in this place? My question to myself and to God was, "Why am I here? I believe in You. I took You as my personal Savior, my Lord and Savior, but I ended up in hell." I did not feel like I belonged there. I felt like I belonged in heaven.

To those who watched me walk by, they would say things like, "You think you're better than us," along with derogatory comments. There was one guy named Sam and another named Richard, and I remember these two because it seemed like they were in a constant argument 24/7. To me, it looked like they had been in an argument ever since they had been in hell. These guys actually knew each other and were on Earth. It was sad that they were still arguing.

I was beginning to get tired. Now I was ready to sit down somewhere and rest, but there was nowhere to rest. The Rock center was so dirty, with burning smoke. There was no sitting on the ground; it was nothing but mud, smoke, and fire. There was no way to lean. It was terrible. I never want to go here again. I was not the only one walking. There were hundreds of thousands of people walking straight down the middle of the street, but God had me turn left, turn left again, turn right, and turn left. He wanted me to see all of these different things and the people that were there. It was unpredictable. It was unbelievable, some of the faces that ended up in hell. All of the money they had was not in a U-Haul truck behind the hearse after the funeral. They had to leave their life on Earth, along with their money, fame, and fortune, and go to a place separated from God for all eternity: hell.

On Earth, it's almost the same visual that you get from a cell in jail or prison. You stand sometimes by yourself, sometimes alone, sometimes in a group of 50.

You are still trapped, eating terrible food, living in close quarters, trapped, bound, forgotten.

Hell is the same way: trapped, bound, forgotten, mad at yourself, mad at your family, mad at your boss, your supervisor, your coworkers, mad at everybody but the people you were mad at. They're not in hell. Most of the people that you're mad at believe in Jesus Christ as their Lord and Savior, and that He went to the cross and died for their sins. He was buried, and on the third day, He got up with all power in His hands. He folded His grave clothes and stepped out of the cemetery, declaring, "All power in heaven and earth is in my hands." He said, "I am He that was dead, yet I am alive forevermore."

I didn't see Jesus in anyone's movie. I saw their sins. I saw the reason why they ended up there. I saw the murders. I saw the kidnappings. I saw the drugs. I saw the human trafficking. I saw the spousal abuse, child abuse. I saw a policeman killing a young black man. I saw the Ku Klux Klan. I saw derogatory groups and gangs, prejudice, and racism. I saw homosexuality and lesbianism. I saw transvestites. I saw confused teenagers. So I kept walking. It seemed like I was getting closer, but the closer I got, when I looked up, the A bridge was so far off, which was frustrating for a lot of people because some of them would take their journey, kind of like when you see refugees crossing over a wall to go into another country illegally. There are groups of them together, and some of them make it, and some of them don't. Some of them come across the ocean, hundreds of them piled on top of each other in boats, trying to get to freedom, trying to get a better life. That's what this was like. It seemed like the people that were walking toward the ~A~ bridge realized that they needed God.

Some of them, but most of them, just wanted to get back to Earth because they realized how good they had it, but they still did not acknowledge God as being in control, as being all-powerful, as being the first and the last, the beginning and the end, the Alpha and the Omega. Some of them were atheists throughout their life and remained the same after they went to hell, refusing to repent. That's the reason why they were there. Over the top of my head, there was smoke rolling like the waves on the sea. There was fire and smoke above my head, and fire and smoke in the little square areas where these people were grouped together according to the sin that does so easily beset them. There was fire everywhere.

Now it seems as if God is relieving me and beginning to interpret this dream to me. I get closer and closer to the ~A~ bridge, and I see these lines of people as if they're at an amusement park, but they're not waiting for a ride. They're not there to have fun. They're trying to get out. This is hell's rumor. Throughout hell, every now and then, a rumor comes up, and people start talking and whispering, wondering if there's any way to get out of this place. Now mind you, no one is preaching the gospel of Jesus Christ, so they don't have any guidance. All they have is rumors. They don't have any leadership; all they have is rumors. So this rumor of the ~A~ bridge comes up and spreads all over hell, and people begin to believe it. They believe that if they can get to the A bridge and get to the very top, they can go back to their life and get another chance—not a second chance, as many people say. How many second chances can you have? They're looking for another chance to do what? I can't tell you because if most of them went back to Earth into their life, they would fall into sin again and would literally have learned nothing from this time that they spent separated from God in this place that the Bible calls hell, also called Hades.

One thing I did not see to this point was satanic beings or Satan's imps or angels. I could feel him. I could hear him, but I could not see him.

So I get to this grassy area that's like corn stalks, real tall over my head, but there was an hour away, and I knew where to walk. I believe the Lord was leading me in which way to go. I could not see Him, but I could feel His presence. When I walked through the stalks, they looked like corn stalks, but it looked like something that was made just for this place called Hell. I walked through, and it seemed like a football field long. I couldn't see to my left and my right; there were no more lots with people in them, no more. It began to lighten up, almost like it was on Earth with the sun, but you know, in this area where they are in Hell, there is no sign. It's all the color of fire, smoky, misty, dark.

So I get to this open area. It's almost like when you take an exhale, although we were still in Hell, it did not look like it. It looked like a different place. So now it seems as if God is relieving me and beginning to interpret the dream to me. I get closer and closer to the ~A~ bridge, and I see these lines of people. It's up there in an amusement park, but they're not waiting for a ride; they're not there to have fun. They're trying to get out. This is Hell's rumor throughout Hell. Every now and then, a rumor comes up, and people start talking and wondering if there's any way to get out of this place. Now, mind you, no one is preaching the gospel of Jesus Christ, so they don't have any guide. The only thing they have are rumors. They don't have any leadership, all they have are rumors. So this rumor of the average comes up and spreads all over Hell, and people begin to believe it and believe that they can get to the bridge and get to the very top. They can go back to their life and get another chance—not a second chance, as many people say. How many second chances can you have? They're looking for another chance to do what? I can tell you, because most of them want to go back to Earth and into their life. They would fall into sin again and would literally have learned nothing from this time spent in separation from God and His place, as the Bible calls Hell, Sheol, Hades.

One thing I did not see up to this point was satanic beings or Satan's angels or demons. I could still hear him, but I could not see him. So I get to this grassy area that's like corn stalks, real tall over my head. Now, from time to time, it seemed that I drifted off and went into another vision—back up to Earth, back to my life—except no one could see me. I could see them, so it seems that I was still dead or a spirit, but I was looking around at the white people living carelessly, as we all lived our lives. When I went back up and saw this, nothing had changed. It was hard for me to tell how long I was in Hell, but it was really sad because I was trying to reach out to the people that were there, but they couldn't hear me or see me. So I watched them, and I began to gather data in my mind to try to see if one day I had an opportunity to preach again or to tell them what good things God has done for their life and how they need to trust in Him. I felt like the beggar in that rich man story. I would reach out to those people in my family that I knew did not acknowledge God, had a mouth full of cursing, and then tried to bless at the same time. They took their money, just threw it away, and never gave that tithe or their offering. Men having children never took care of them. And I saw all of this stuff that we have at our fingertips that we can do against God and against His will, and how the enemy whispers. The only thing he whispers is sometimes because he doesn't need to do a whole lot of work. We have so much evil and devilish things inside of us that we want to do, he just has an easy job. But then there are those that really love God and are called according to His purpose. But they may have circumstances in their life, like Job, that may have Hell coming at them from every side. They may have sickness in their body or in their families. They may have sickness in their family, disease, and folks in the hospital. And people that trust God and are going to church still suffer. And in these things happening, while folks are down in Hell and they're burning continually, I'm sorry, I heard they're away from God.

So while I was in this vision or dream or this place, I remember everything that happened while I was down in hell. And while I was there, back on earth again, I asked God to give me another chance to preach better, to pray better, to evangelize better, to heal the sick better.

God, I was thanking Him for all that He did for me in my life, even the little things, even the moments of poverty that I went through, and indecision, the depression, and oppression. I was thanking God for every single thing that was in my life because I saw the desperation in the cry that went forth in hell and how it was dark and grimy and sexy and hot and fiery and sweaty and stinky and nasty. It was a place where nobody respected anybody, and there were a lot of rumors going on because nobody wanted to be there. No one believed that they had to be there for eternity, but the truth of the matter is that they were going to spend the rest of eternity separated from God, pulling on chains, standing in the mud and dirt, and such, and remembering the craziness they did in their life, and how they could have given their life to Christ, they could have received Him in their heart, they could have, hallelujah, resurrected their lives like never before. But we didn't trust God, we didn't trust Jesus. We thought that it was just a fantasy or fallacy. Many of us were talked into being Jehovah's Witnesses, and some were Muslims, and some were Hindus, and some, hallelujah, followed crazy religions and motorcycle gangs and all kinds of nonsense, having sex and spreading disease and babies out of wedlock. We were just having a ball, and then all of a sudden I was back in hell, looking at the reality of jealousy, bitterness, disobedience—how we read the words sometimes but didn't believe it was God speaking. All of these people down here dressed up, looking like they used to be CEOs of companies. None of them had money behind that hearse, other than a U-Haul truck to bring all of the riches that they accumulated during their life. None of that stuff came with them to hell. The only thing that came with them to hell is the past and their decision to mock God, to call Him all kinds of names, and to spit on Jesus and pull His beard and hang Him on the cross, as if, hallelujah, that would destroy Him. It made Him stronger where He was weak, He was strong in His Father's arms. And now I'm down in hell and I've got all this word inside of me, why can't I save anybody? And so God said, "Take me back to the top of the bridge," and I looked back towards the cliff where I started my journey, and I saw all of these people coming, crowds and trolls, just crying out and not knowing how they were going to make it, but they knew they had to get to the bridge. And it was so sad because all of their strength and pain and suffering were used to try to make it to this long trek to this distant place that someone started a rumor saying that if we get there, we can go back to our life, and we get another chance to try and get it right.

Having sex, spreading disease, and having babies out

of wedlock—it was like we were just having a ball, and then all of a sudden, I was back in Hell, looking at the reality of jealousy, bitterness, and disobedience and how we need to read the word sometimes, but we didn't believe it was God speaking. All of these people down here, dressed up looking like they used to be CEOs of companies, and none of them had money behind them. It hurts, and none of them had a U-Haul truck to bring all of the riches that they accumulated during their life. None of that stuff came with them to Hell. The only thing that came with them to Hell is the pastor that led them astray and the decision to mock my God, to call Him all kinds of names, and to spit on Him.

There was a young man in Hell, his name was Jerry. Jerry kept calling my name, kept calling my name, and mentioning things that happened in my life so I would know that he knew who I was. You know the power that God has given me. He knew that I had raised the dead before. Can I feed the hungry? Can I heal the sick? Because the anointing of Jesus Christ was on my life, the anointing that removes burdens and destroys yokes. So Jerry kept talking, and he kept talking, and while he was talking to me, he was talking to someone else in another lot, that rented lot that had about 30 people in this very small area, and they were confined and chained in this spot. Jerry was talking to them about me and all the stuff that I had done in my life.

Jerry was talking to them about a lot of stuff that I did in my life, vices that I had, that sin that does so easily beset me. And his point was he was comparing my life because he knew that eventually, I would leave Hell and go back to my life. He knew somehow that I was just a visitor, that God was showing me something because He wanted me to preach to His people and let them know that Hell is real, that the ~A~ bridge is a rumor, and that there is no second chance after you have denied Christ and have not received Him as your Lord and Savior. You don't get another chance. So Jerry kept talking. He mentioned something to this young lady named Janica. So he was telling Janica, "Well, what you've done isn't that bad because look what he's done, and he got saved, and he got set free, and he got renewed and revived and replenished. Look at him." So they compared notes and began to look at different people's lives because their lives and their sins were showing up on the screen. And so this area, these lots, where there were several people—some lots had 10, 20, 30 people—all of a sudden, it was like a fiery red, and there was fire over the top of their heads just rolling. It was so hot, everybody was sweating and fussing and cussing. There was no peace, it was just all chaotic, nothing but chaos.

And so this young man, Jerry, began to talk to other people, screaming across lots and telling people to look at their lives and the things that they had done against God and compare them to how I lived my life and what I had on my screen. It was deep. I mean, people in Hell were saying, "Why are we in Hell? Why isn't he in Hell?" And it was a trip. And so God began walking with me back down the streets. I went down different streets this time, turning right, turning left, stopping at some. It seemed like the Lord wanted me to see a lot of different circumstances, a lot of different types of people, and a lot of different levels of financial prosperity that they had while they were living.

So we kept walking, and then it seemed like the Lord was pushing me to begin running. And while I was running, it became harder to hear what Jerry was saying because he was further and further back. And so the conversation shifted from Jerry to Larry, who was part of another group that committed other kinds of sins. And Larry started looking at my movie, at my life, at the way I lived, how I loved God. Even though I loved God, I did something wrong. I had a record, I went through some stuff, I've been to jail, I did some stuff, I got divorced, I slept around when I was younger, I did a lot of crazy stuff. And if you looked at my movie, you would say, "There is no way he's going to Heaven." That's when I remember what God did for me. They can't remember, all they remember is their sins. It's how they felt about God, how they worked tirelessly to pull people away from God and not believe in Him. They couldn't see what I saw. They saw my mistakes and mishaps. They saw my sins and transgressions. I saw the blood of Jesus covering every dumb decision that I made, every bad move, every dime that was stolen, every curse word that came out of my mouth, every woman that I had sex with.

And so Larry began to talk to this young lady named Donnetta. You could tell Donnetta was beautiful at one time. She was not like the other women that were in Hell. Their faces seemed to be very scarred up and dirty, full of dirt and soot.

But I never seem to be flashing back and remembering all of the opportunities that she had to receive Jesus in her life. No one else could see this, but Dinetah began to see young people that crossed our path and began to talk about God and how she changed the subject. Oftentimes, she would take people's minds off of anything spiritual, especially anything dealing with Christianity. She had been talked to many times by other religions. While we were walking back towards the beginning of this journey that I was on, I saw that she began to see all the times that she went to church, all the times that her mind was on something else, all the times when the preacher came down and gave the invitation to Christ, how she changed her mind, changed, and she began to think evil thoughts. It seemed like every time she went to church, she never heard him say, "Come to Christ." It was always blotted out by something else in her mind—something somebody was saying to her, a question being asked during the service, the music. She blocked out the music because they were singing about Jesus. She thought it was silly. So she began seeing this movie of all the opportunities she had during her life. She died at 26. It was so sad. She had two children, a husband, and she died of a disease. While she was sick, there was no prayer in our life. Other people were praying for her, but she never crossed their path. They had heard of her sickness, and they prayed, and they prayed. But sometimes you can pray, and it just seems to hit the wall. Why? Because the person you're praying for doesn't have faith, or the person you're praying for is not a child of God, or the person you're praying for has blocked out God. And we know that all things work together for the good to them that love God and are the called according to His purpose. So Dinetah began to weep, and it's almost as if she wanted to tell everybody that we're not here because God is so bad. We're here because God is just. He gave all of us an opportunity to receive what Jesus Christ cried out on Calvary when He said, "It is finished." It was amazing. It was as if Dinetah had been overtaken by the Holy Spirit while she was in hell. I don't know how to explain it. God didn't explain it to me, nor all the interpretation of this moment in time, this journey I was on, walking through hell, practically living in hell. He never said anything about Dinetah, and I'm wondering if Dinetah was saying what she was saying because God wanted them to know what time is. Settle on life eternal in the bosom of our Father. I remember they used to say in church all the time, "He came that we might have life, and life more abundantly." Many of us lived in poverty and depression, not because it was our destiny, but because we did not have faith in what God said about us. He said He would never leave us nor forsake us. He said that He had given us the power to get wealth. He said He wanted our soul to prosper and for us to be in good health.

It was amazing because I could feel God right next to me. It was almost like I could feel Him brush up against my arm. I couldn't see Him, but I knew He was there, and His presence was so thick. But I don't believe anybody else that was in hell could see Him, feel Him, hear Him, or know that He was there because it was so dark, and it was so sad, terrible. So as we began to get closer and closer to what I called the cliff, to where I started off this journey toward the Lord, He pushed me off, and I fell down onto the fire. I began to hear all of the noise in the weeping and gnashing of teeth that the Bible talks about. Why is there weeping and gnashing? Well, from what I saw, it's because everything is dark, dreary, smoky, fiery, and hot, and there's no relief. It's constant because you're separated from God.

So many of them repeat negative things that happened in her life over and over again—negative situations, pain, problems, ridiculous therapy, like on a video, over and over and over again. And on top of that, their skin is burning continuously, like someone has held an iron under their skin, and it kills off at the top of the cry out. They believe that they can leave this area, this place, little pain, if they get to the average. It is so sad: millionaires, big business people, athletes with millions of dollars, while they were in their life on Earth, are now in hell. There are people who thought that they were going to heaven but ended up in hell, and the Lord told them, "I never knew you," which means they never really accepted Jesus as their Savior. You can't fake it, you can't trick Him, you can't fool God. This place is terrible. I wouldn't want anyone to have to experience this. It's like a big junkyard full of fire, mud, and a foul smell.

Now I see I will be going back, turning my life before the heart attack, and I see all these cars going up and down the street. It looks like New York City. On each corner of every block, there's at least one person who is contemplating taking their own life. So you might wonder why we jump from the scene in hell back to Earth to deal with those who may not want to live anymore—those who are thinking about throwing themselves in front of a car or taking a gun and blowing their head off, those who are fed up with life, those who have gone through so many things, so much abuse, so much ridicule, and some are just people who have low self-esteem. Regardless of why they are there, we still have to find a way to change their minds and turn them around, to let them know that God loves them, that Jesus died for them, and that they have a reason to live, that they were created for such a time as this. There is too much potential, power, and purpose for them to pursue their goals in life. Their lives are so precious, so we must reach out and let them know that all things work together for the good to them that love God and are the called according to His purpose.

This is why the prophetic anointing and call are crucial during these times. People with a true prophetic call can guide and forth-tell and give a word of knowledge to change the direction that Satan has convinced a person to go.

So I look out and I see thousands of people walking across the street in New York. I don't know what part of New York it is, but I see on every corner, on every block, at least one person ready to give up. And so what we do, because we know the location of these people, is we can pray specifically and strategically, and we can find a way to save their life and their soul, snatching them from the fire of eternal damnation. And also, their families from the hurt, anguish, and shame of suicide.

Let's not celebrate. There are many people going through this life and making it into their adult years without ever really being taught the gospel of Jesus Christ, and that it has the power of God unto salvation to those who believe. Look, we prayed for everyone on every corner in this city of New York, and guess what happened? People began to turn around, look at their phones, head back home, change their mind, and find a reason to hear a phone call or voice message with someone telling them that they are significant and that they are worth the blessing of God and His salvation. And that they have potential, power, and purpose for survival.

Bless the name of Jesus because of our prayer, our

fervent, strategic prayer that was sent out on every corner of this city in New York. Thousands of people's lives were saved. Why the sidebar? Why this addendum? Because the reason for this book, the reason for this research, and the reason for this trip to Hell is to let people know that God is real and that He is a rewarder of them that diligently seek Him. And so I thought about all of the people already in Hell, and all of the people who were prominent while they were here on Earth—CEOs of companies, business people, philanthropists, and powerful men and women in politics who gave to the poor but still ended up separated from God for eternity. Now why is that? Simply because they would not submit, believe, and follow our Lord and Savior Jesus Christ, who is and was and is to come, the Almighty. Yes, that is why!

I leave this area in New York where all of these people are walking the streets, going to work, lunch, dinner, meetings, and I'm transported to an area on the other side of the country. It looks like I am now in North Carolina, and there is a big mall in this city, which I can't name. This mall is huge.

I walk into the mall and see so many people: young, old, black, white, Asian, Jewish, Muslim, and Christian.

I wondered why God had me there, so I began walking in the mall and seeing things I wanted to buy. I forgot that I was on a fishing trip, but I really didn't know what the mission was. I just knew that there were a lot of people. Now, in that area of New York where I was, there were many people, including those contemplating suicide. I wondered if God sent me to this mall because there is a dilemma, a problem, a predicament, and it does so easily beset us that it may hinder some of these people from receiving God.

There was a huge escalator in front of me that had a waterfall coming down. It was about maybe 60 or 70 feet in the air. It was beautiful, so I got on this escalator and began to go up. I saw all of these people just basking in this beautiful area of the mall and enjoying it. Then, I saw on the other side of the escalator going down, some kids running and chasing each other. By the time they got to the bottom, three of them fell. One of them had his face on the escalator steps, and people were stepping on him. Finally, they got to the bottom and were fatally injured, and many people that were on the escalator were injured.

So, I went up to the top of the escalator and took the stairway down to see if I could help. I was running fast, so I almost tripped and fell myself. By the time I got there, there were security and EMS trying to help these kids. A couple of them had bruised ribs and were having problems breathing, so they were doing CPR. Others that were injured on the escalator going down were sitting in chairs in the food court and being taken care of by some of the mall personnel and those around who wanted to help. So, what was my place? What could I do? It seemed like they all had helped, so I began to pray. I began to pray out loud over in the food court, and people began to circle around me. It seemed like a little innocent accident, but people really got hurt badly from this fall because the escalator was so tall. Like I said, the waterfall coming down from it was at least 70 feet in the air. Some of the people were taken out to the ambulance, and some were administered care right there in the mall.

So, we got our logo together. We didn't know each other, but we knew a guy who could take care of any problem or situation. It just so happened that one of the children who were running and chasing each other, having fun, was having a hard time breathing, and I needed to rush him to the hospital because he hit his head. Also, he's the one who hit his head on the escalator steps, and you know how those are made of metal. It seemed like what was going on in this mall with these kids had nothing to do with anything, but it's amazing how God orchestrates these events. Things happen, problems come up, circumstances arise; He gives us the answers, and we are able to make decisions. On top of that, He has a work for us to find out how He feels about a particular problem or predicament that we're in. He gives us the answer for everything we need in His Word, and it hurts my heart to think that anyone who is on this earth right now could not understand and believe that God is a loving God, that He's a true God, and that He has made a way of escape for all of us.

So I sit here now, how many seats the reclining chair in the hospital TV blasting, at peace with myself and with God, being told today that the way it's been made in the schedule, it's been open for me to have quadruple bypass surgery. It is so amazing that this situation and this project and me writing this book all came because I was sitting on my bed. I saw myself dead. I had a heart attack. I left my body. I believe in God. I believe Jesus Christ died and was risen from the dead by God Almighty.

When I died, I went to Hell. I don't want anybody to ever experience what God showed me concerning this place where there's separation from God for eternity, where there's weeping and gnashing of teeth, for this complaining and bickering and blaming. What a terrible place. So, as I sit here a week or so after having a heart attack, almost losing my life several times within the past few months, I know it's necessary for me to finish this book, for me to let people know that Heaven and Hell are real.

So, when I say real, what do I really mean? What I mean is, for example, there was a guy that owned this company. He was the founder. He loved this company, and with blood, sweat, and tears, he built the foundation. He began to hire different college graduates who excelled in their major and were top in their class.

Jerry gave these college students great opportunities to excel in his company and to be creative, how to grow the company. He began to hire others that were not college students. Some were in college, and some were just great workers with great resumes. So, the company began to grow, excel, and make mega money, and Jerry began to move away from the executive office and begin purchasing other businesses.

Jerry was just a phenomenal businessman with great ideas, great intuition, great discernment, and a knack for finding faithful people as employees. It seemed Jerry never got the big head because of his accomplishments. He was always trying to help somebody better themselves, never really sarcastic. He corrected mistakes, but very rarely.

Jerry was kind of boring, but he was precise, and he pursued his purpose. And you knew what he was about when you met him. He didn't play; he was about business. So, you say to yourself, why am I telling you about the great life Jerry had and the phenomenal business that he created? It's because, out of all the great things that Jerry had done, Jerry never got married and never had any children. He never had a chance to share the great things that he accomplished in his life with anyone except his family. He wasn't really close to family, although he was always there when someone needed help.

The strange thing about Jerry was you never heard him talk about God. You never heard him give God credit for anything. He never bragged much about what he did, but he would let you know that he was an atheist and he did not believe in God nor the fact that Jesus died for our sins. Now, the story gets interesting.

Jerry went to the gym and was playing racquetball with a couple of guys, and there were some females who wanted to join them. So, they began playing two on two, having fun, going at it, competing, and finally calling it quits after the women whipped them. Jerry was laughing because before this, he thought he could play. One of the young ladies began flirting with him. They went outside the court and got some water, began talking, laughing, and they got along very well. Jerry's friend Bobby was talking to the other young lady, and they hit it off also. They both agreed to meet a little bit later.

Jerry and the young lady, whose name was Carol, began to talk about where they came from, their background, and how they grew up. They found out they had a lot in common, and they began laughing, mainly because Jerry was in his mid-forties and he was single, but he didn't mention his financial background or how well-off he was.

He didn't lie, but he didn't share everything. He was really modest, and Carol really liked him. So they talked about going to get some ice cream. He texted his buddy Bobby and told him that Carol was about to take him for a ride to get some ice cream.

They went to the parking lot, and as it happened, they were parked one car away from each other. Jerry was driving a Bentley, and Carol was in a BMW, a nice one, one of the big 700 series. So they both agreed to go in Jerry's car to the ice cream store, which was not too far. They got in the car, Bobby and Shona opened the door, they pulled off, and began laughing about how badly the women beat them in handball/racquetball. They decided to go to this place called Menchie's, real good yogurt, looks like ice cream, tastes better. So he pulled up, went into Menchie's, and began to look around at the different flavors. Jerry loved strawberry, so he got a mixture of strawberry, vanilla, grape, and pineapple. Now, in Menchie's, you pay according to how much your bowl weighs. His was $5 by itself. They were laughing, hers came to about $2.50. They wanted to sit outside, so they found a seat outside and began to talk. Carol was beautiful, sexy, fun, and very smart. Jerry was definitely interested, and he said, "Today, I had a pretty good time," and they headed back to the gym, exchanged numbers, and planned on seeing each other again. Jerry hugged her and kissed her on the cheek, and then she kissed him on the lips and smiled and said, "I beat you twice today." He opened her car door, and she got in. Then he got in his car and waited for her to pull off.

Not once during that visit did he mention the kind of work he did or how much money he made, nor did he brag about his life and how he was driving a Bentley, but that never came up with either of them; they just liked each other's company and time.

Jerry is a good guy, and Carol is a very nice girl. Now, remember I told you that Jerry was pushing away from the executive position in his company and starting to purchase other businesses. It just so happens that the company Carol worked for was one of the companies that was up for bid that Jerry was interested in. Although he had no idea that she worked there. Both of them lead very busy lives and had very little time, especially for dating and all that it takes to keep a relation-ship together.

Jerry proceeded with his bid to purchase this company. He got all of his contracts and paperwork together to make his offer, and the time came on the following week, on Friday, when he approached the executive branch of this company. Now, there were some things going on with this company, or they felt that they were on a downward spiral, but Jerry could see some potential and how he could multiply and make this place flourish. Although this organization had so much debt, it looked like a bad move.

On the other hand, Carol went to work every day; she was on salary, so she spent a lot of time at work. She was one of the company's top employees. She didn't know that the executive branch of this company decided to cut back, getting rid of some positions, consolidating, and laying people off.

Wouldn't you know that Carol was one of the first ones on the list, because of her salary, to be laid off? They were about to let her go and several others—people that had families, bills, and obligations. Meanwhile, the meeting was called, and Jerry was going to lay out his offer in an attempt to take over this company.

He wasn't worried about who was staying and who was leaving; his main goal was to flip the script and turn this place around. Whatever it took to do that was his main objective. He was experienced at this kind of takeover. He had been doing this type of thing a long time; he was a very successful businessman.

Carol was called into a board meeting, and there were about 10 other employees, managers, and supervisors at the table. The CEO began to explain how things suddenly started going in a downward spiral with their business. Because of the competition, they were forced to send a lot of the jobs overseas, and they had to make some changes immediately.

Because of the hard work and dedication that had been made by the people at the table, he explained how hard it was to make these decisions and also why they needed to be made. While the CEO was holding this meeting, there was another meeting going on. The flooring office had missed Jerry making his offer, and branches were contemplating taking this off the table, but the CEO was letting people go at that very same moment.

Towards the end of the meeting, the CEO passed out a package for each one at the table, a severance package to hold them over until they could find something else. While he was in the midst of passing these papers out and giving them their package, he got a call to come downstairs to another meeting, told everyone he wasn't finished, concluded his talk, and said that they would reconnect later. Jerry and Carol were in the same building at the same company, one floor separated them. The CEO of the company was about to step into a meeting with the executive branch and businessmen who wanted to buy their company. Jerry's offer was on the table and was accepted by the view board from the executive branch, and the only thing that was needed to move forward was the signature of the chief executive officer and founder of this company.

Everyone went back to their desks, some in shock, some expecting something to happen; for the most part, everyone knew that a change was about to happen and some of their lives would be changed forever. Some of them had spent most of their lives with this company. Some were mad, some were grateful, but the one who had excelled the most in this season was Carol. She was in shock; she couldn't believe that they were going to let her go. So, the president of the top executive branch stood up and made an announcement. He talked about Jerry, introduced him, and laid down his offer. The CEO was in shock; he wanted to bring in investors to help but just could not bring himself to finalize any deals. Jerry's offer was actually amazing; he had offered enough money to get them out of debt, and also a way to keep most of the important pieces in place (some of the executive officers).

The CEO said that he wanted to talk to his lawyer and look over the paperwork. Jerry gave him two days to make a decision. "Are you in for the offer on the table?" "Yes," he said, "I am in," with a smile on his face. One day passed, and the CEO met with his lawyers. They looked over the paperwork; for some reason, they were kind of skeptical, but they ultimately agreed that it was a good deal. The CEO called Jerry back himself. He didn't send a secretary to do it or one of his assistants; he made the call himself. The phone rang, and Jerry answered the phone very calm, cool, and collected.

Jerry answered, "Hello." The CEO responded, "Let's do this." Jerry's response was, "Okay, when do you want to meet?" The CEO said, "Later this evening around 5 p.m."

The offer was accepted; there was no barter, no going back and forth. Paperwork was signed, the deal was made, and the transition began. Once the announcement was made to all the employees of the company, there was a hush for a long time. Oftentimes, the CEO didn't say anything; he did not let them know upfront who would be kept and who would ultimately lose their job. But he felt he was doing the right thing, and getting the company's name out of debt was his most important mission right now. The funny thing about the whole transaction between the CEO and Jerry was that all of Jerry's life, he had always been in a position to help people get out of trouble, but he did not know then that one of the employees who was about to be laid off was the young lady he had met weeks ago.

Remember, they went out to dinner; they had such a great time, and they really liked each other. Deep down, this conversation that they needed to have never happened. She was a devout Christian, and he was an atheist, so now what? The strange thing is, while they were both in the same building, they never crossed paths, and the name of the buyer was never mentioned. When the CEO mentioned the buyer and new owner, it was by his company name.

Jerry was so happy that the deal was done that he called his new friend Carol to let her know that he had some free time if she wanted to connect. He picked up his cell and dialed her number, and the phone rang several times, but Carol did not pick up. Jerry didn't think anything was wrong, but at this moment, Carol was struggling because of the devastating news she had just received from her job.

Jerry decided to try and call her back in about 15 minutes. After he waited, he called her back, and the phone rang six times. On the seventh ring, he was about to hang up when she answered with a different voice.

"Hello," Carol said.

Then Jerry said, "Hey there, how was your day?"

Carol was evasive and said, "It was okay."

Jerry said, "Great," but he ignored her tone and asked her to meet him down by the lake. She said, "Okay." So they got off the phone and both got into their cars to meet up.

Jerry arrived first, but he remembered that he forgot to tell Carol where to meet him. He began to dial her number and heard a phone ringing in the car behind him—and it was hers. Carol found the spot without him even telling her.

"LOL, you are something else," Jerry said, and Carol smiled and put her head down.

Jerry noticed a sadness in her countenance and asked her what was wrong.

He said, "Hey baby, you are not your cheerful self."

She didn't say anything. She just laid her head on his chest and began crying. Jerry put his hand on her head and said, "I got chu, baby." Jerry didn't press her for info about the problem.

Finally, she loosened up and said, "I was there so long, and I was one of the top employees, and they gave me a big raise, but they let me go today."

Now, remember—they never talked about their jobs before, so Jerry was stunned.

Carol said, "They let me go."

Jerry said, "Wow, no way."

He said, "Carol, I am so sorry."

She stepped back and asked Jerry if he could pray with her.

Jerry had this blank look on his face, and he stepped back also and said, "I am so sorry, but you probably want to call one of your other friends because I don't pray."

She said, "I never told you, but I am a Christian, and I believe in God."

And Jerry said, "Wow, this is a trip."

She said, "What's a trip?"

Jerry said, "We started liking each other without asking some of the most important questions."

"So what do you believe?" Carol asked very timidly.

And Jerry said, "I don't really believe in anything. I definitely am an atheist."

She responded, "No way!"

And he said, "Yes way, so I can't pray with you. You know, it's funny—I brought you out here to share with you what happened today. I have been in business for about 20 years, and often I research other businesses and properties to purchase. So today, I put in a bid for a company, and it was accepted. I WAS SO EXCITED THAT I WANTED TO SHARE THE NEWS WITH YOU."

Carol looked at him with a strange look on her face, one that was not necessarily a happy one. Why? Because Jerry changed the subject so fast to talk about something totally different. She was asking him about his faith, and he didn't even believe in God.

So Carol heard him, but she wasn't listening. She was upset because it seemed like her problem did not matter anymore.

Jerry stopped and said, "I am so sorry, but I can't and won't pray with you. There is another way to handle your issue. I could loan you some money if that becomes a problem. But praying to a God that doesn't exist is not the way to resolve this."

Carol hugged Jerry and, in silence, got into her car and pulled off.

The question is, how do you deal with a situation like this if you are a believer in God and what Jesus Christ cried out on Calvary, saying, "It is finished."

Now what?

I think I love him already, but it doesn't matter how much money he has or what he is driving—if a man cannot pray for me, he is not my man.

Wow, I am undone. He was such a nice guy, and the

sad thing is, with all that he has going for him, when he dies and leaves here, he will end up in HELL with all the other non-believers and CEOs, and movie stars, and singers, and politicians, and NFL STARS THAT DON'T BELIEVE THAT JESUS CHRIST IS THE ONLY WAY, THE TRUTH, AND THE LIFE AND THAT NO MAN COMES UNTO THE FATHER BUT BY HIM.

I cannot continue this story without letting you decide what you would do. Would you move forward with this relationship, knowing this person does not share your faith? Or would you take a chance, following your desires, hoping that one day he would receive Jesus as Lord and Savior?

Some people enter marriages with partners they know are not saved, hoping that one day they will come to accept God's word and His way. But light and darkness cannot dwell together. The Gospel of John says:

"Yet to all who did receive him, to those who believed in his name, he gave the right to become children of God." (John 1:12)

I prophesy to you right now: If you don't stand for something, you will fall for anything—even if it is evil and designed to steal, kill, or destroy you. God is not mocked. Whatever a man sows, that shall he also reap.

I declare that opportunities will arise in the coming months where you will be faced with choices beyond laughter, romance, love, and marriage. If you join your-self with someone who is not saved, it could destroy your home and your business. Don't be like Jerry—accomplished in the world but lost in his soul.

Remember: *The Bridge was Hell's rumor. There is no way to be forgiven once you lose your salvation. Hell is real. Don't go!*

God has said that many churches today are drawing people in with gimmicks and schemes. But the Holy Ghost has all the power needed to draw souls to Christ. Share the gospel and offer Jesus. If they reject Him, then offer them your church. You plant the seed, someone else waters it, and God gives the increase.

Shalom,
Prophet Brandon L. Davis
soonerthanrightnow@yahoo.com
Follow me on YouTube: **Prophet Brandon L**

PART II

BONUS / WORKBOOK

5

LOVE IS ON THE WAY, NOW WHAT?

Jerry and Carol met at a charity event for a local animal shelter. Jerry was immediately drawn to Carol's warm smile and kind eyes. They struck up a conversation and quickly discovered they had a lot in common. They both loved animals, enjoyed hiking, and had a passion for helping others.

As they spent more time together, Jerry and Carol found themselves falling in love. They enjoyed long walks in the park, cozy dinners by the fire, and lazy Sunday mornings in bed. They shared their hopes and dreams, their fears and insecurities, and their deepest desires.

But as their relationship deepened, they began to uncover some differences that threatened to tear them apart. Carol was a devout Christian, while Jerry was an atheist. They had never discussed religion before, assuming it was a non-issue. But now, it loomed large between them, casting a shadow over their budding romance.

One evening, as they sat on the couch watching a movie, Carol turned to Jerry and said, "I need to talk to you about something important."

Jerry looked at her, concern etched on his face. "What is it, Carol? You can tell me anything."

Carol took a deep breath. "I'm a Christian, Jerry. My faith is a big part of who I am. I go to church every Sunday, I pray every day, and I believe in God with all my heart."

Jerry's heart sank. He had never been a religious person, and the idea of dating someone so devout was daunting. "I'm an atheist, Carol," he said quietly. "I don't believe in God. I believe in science and reason."

Carol looked at him, her eyes filled with sadness. "I know, Jerry. And I respect your beliefs. But this is important to me. I can't imagine being with someone who doesn't share my faith."

Jerry felt a lump form in his throat. He had never felt this way about anyone before, and the thought of losing Carol was unbearable. "I love you, Carol," he said, his voice trembling. "I don't want to lose you."

Carol reached out and took his hand. "I love you too,

Jerry. But we have to be honest with each other. We can't ignore this difference between us. It's too important."

They sat in silence for a moment, the weight of their words hanging heavy in the air. Finally, Jerry spoke. "I don't know what to do, Carol. I don't want to lose you, but I don't know if I can change my beliefs."

Carol squeezed his hand. "I don't want you to change, Jerry. I just want us to be honest with each other. Maybe we can find a way to make this work. Maybe we can learn from each other and grow together."

Jerry looked into her eyes, seeing the love and understanding there. "I want to try, Carol. I want to be with you, no matter what."

And so, Jerry and Carol embarked on a journey of love and discovery, navigating the complexities of faith and belief. They learned to respect each other's differences, to listen and learn, and to grow together as a couple. In the end, they found that love was stronger than any obstacle and that faith could be a bridge, not a barrier, between them. Jerry finally confessed his faith in Jesus Christ as Lord and Savior.

6

THE AWAKENING | STAY FAITHFUL UNTO GOD

As the sun rose over the small town of Willow Creek, Sarah sat on her porch, sipping her morning coffee and reflecting on the sermon she had heard at church the day before. The pastor had spoken about the importance of being faithful to God and following His commandments. Sarah couldn't help but feel a sense of unease as she thought about her own life and the choices she had made.

She had always considered herself a good person, someone who tried to do the right thing and help others whenever she could. But as she listened to the pastor's words, she couldn't shake the feeling that there was something missing in her life—something she had been neglecting.

As she sat there, lost in thought, a voice interrupted

her reverie. "Good morning, Sarah," said a familiar voice. Sarah looked up to see her neighbor, John, standing at the fence that separated their properties. John was a kind and gentle man, someone who always had a smile on his face and a kind word for everyone he met.

"Good morning, John," Sarah replied, forcing a smile. "How are you today?"

"I'm doing well, thank you," John said, his eyes filled with concern. "I couldn't help but notice that you seem troubled. Is everything okay?"

Sarah hesitated for a moment, unsure of how to respond. She had always kept her thoughts and feelings to herself, afraid of being judged or criticized. But something about John's gentle demeanor made her want to open up to him.

"I... I don't know, John," Sarah said, her voice barely above a whisper. "I've been thinking a lot about my faith lately, about whether I'm truly living according to God's will."

John nodded understandingly, his eyes filled with compassion. "I think we all struggle with that from time to time, Sarah," he said. "But the important thing is to remember that God is always there for us, ready to forgive us and guide us back onto the right path."

Sarah felt a sense of relief wash over her as she listened to John's words. For the first time in a long time, she felt a glimmer of hope that she could find peace and redemption in her faith.

"Thank you, John," Sarah said, her voice filled with gratitude. "I needed to hear that today."

John smiled warmly at her, his eyes shining with kindness. "Anytime, Sarah," he said. "We're all in this together, trying to navigate the challenges of life and find our way back to God's love."

As Sarah watched John walk back to his house, she felt a sense of peace settle over her. She knew that the road ahead would be difficult, filled with obstacles and temptations. But with God's guidance and the support of her friends and neighbors, she knew that she could find the strength to stay faithful and true to her beliefs.

And as she closed her eyes and whispered a prayer of thanks, she felt a sense of hope and renewal fill her heart. For in the end, she knew that God's love would always be there, waiting for her to come home.

7

WALKING THROUGH HELL

I couldn't believe what I was seeing and hearing in hell—the screams of agony, the smell of sulfur, the intense heat that seemed to sear my very soul. I saw people I knew, people I had admired and looked up to, suffering for eternity. It was a terrifying and sobering experience.

As I stood there, feeling helpless and overwhelmed, a voice spoke to me. It was a voice filled with love and compassion, yet also with a sense of urgency. It was the voice of God, and He told me that I had been given this out-of-body experience for a reason. He wanted me to go back to Earth and share the message of salvation with His church.

I was filled with a sense of purpose and determination. I knew that I had to do whatever it took to spread the word of God and to warn others of the reality of hell. I returned to my body with a newfound sense of urgency and passion.

I began to speak to anyone who would listen, sharing my experience and the message that God had given me. Some people scoffed and dismissed me as a fanatic, but others listened with open hearts and minds. I saw lives transformed and hearts changed as people came to know the love and grace of God.

Through it all, I never forgot the sights and sounds of hell. It was a constant reminder of the reality of sin and the consequences of rejecting God. But it also served as a reminder of the incredible love and mercy of God, who had given me a second chance to share His message with the world.

As I continued on my journey, I found myself drawn to a young woman who had also experienced a similar out-of-body experience. We bonded over our shared experiences and our shared faith, and before long, we fell deeply in love.

Our love story was one of faith, hope, and redemption. We faced challenges and obstacles, but we always knew that God was with us, guiding us and protecting us. Our love grew stronger with each passing day, and we knew that we were meant to be together.

In the end, our love story was a testament to the

power of God's love and grace. We had both been given a second chance—no, actually, we were given another chance—and we were determined to make the most of it. As we walked hand in hand into the future, we knew that God's love would always be with us, guiding us and protecting us every step of the way.

8

THE COFFEE SHOP

THE COFFEE SHOP

As Sarah walked through the bustling city streets, her heart was heavy with the weight of the world. She had always been a woman of faith, relying on God's word to guide her through life's challenges. But lately, she had been struggling to keep her thoughts pure and her actions in line with her beliefs.

She knew that the key to walking by faith and not by sight was to keep God's word in her heart, to meditate on it day and night. She knew that the more she immersed herself in the scriptures, the more she would be able to resist temptation and live a life pleasing to God.

But it was easier said than done. The pressures of the world, the distractions of everyday life—they all seemed to conspire against her. She found herself slipping, giving in to anger, jealousy, and pride. She knew that she needed to do better, to be better.

One day, as she sat in her favorite coffee shop, a young man approached her. His name was Michael, and he had a kind smile and a gentle spirit. They struck up a conversation, and before long, Sarah found herself opening up to him about her struggles.

Michael listened intently, his eyes filled with compassion. Then, he began to speak to her about the power of God's love, the sacrifice of Jesus Christ, and the hope and redemption available to all who believed.

Sarah felt a stirring in her heart, a glimmer of hope. She knew that she had strayed from the path, but she also knew that God's grace was greater than her sin. She knew that she could start anew, that she could be forgiven and restored.

And so, with Michael's guidance, she began to immerse herself once again in the scriptures. She read the words of Romans, letting them sink deep into her soul. She confessed her sins, asking for forgiveness and cleansing. She prayed for strength and guidance, for a renewed spirit and a steadfast heart.

And as she walked by faith, not by sight, she felt a peace and a joy that she had not known in a long time. She knew that she still had a long way to go, that she would stumble and fall along the way. But she also knew that God was with her, that His love would never fail her.

And as she looked into Michael's eyes, she knew that she had found a kindred spirit, a fellow traveler on the journey of faith. Together, they would walk hand in hand, keeping God's word in their hearts and sharing His love with all they met.

9

SOUL WINNERS

The sun was setting over the city as I stood on the bridge, looking out at the river below. It was a peaceful evening, the sound of the water flowing gently, soothing my troubled mind. I had come to this bridge many times over the past few months, seeking solace and peace in the midst of the chaos that had become my life.

As I stood there, lost in my thoughts, I heard footsteps approaching from behind me. I turned to see a man walking toward me, a warm smile on his face. It was Brother Kenny, the evangelist who had become a mentor and friend to me during my time in Nashville.

"Hey there, sister," he said, his voice filled with kindness. "Mind if I join you?"

I nodded, grateful for his presence. We stood

together in silence for a few moments, watching the sun dip below the horizon. Then, Brother Kenny spoke.

"I know you've been through a lot, sister," he said, his eyes filled with compassion. "But remember, God has a plan for you. He's using you in ways you can't even imagine."

I felt tears welling up in my eyes as I thought about all the pain and heartache I had experienced in recent months—my divorce, the separation from my son, the struggles I faced every day. But Brother Kenny's words reminded me that God was still with me, guiding me through the darkness.

"I know it's hard to share the gospel with family and friends," Brother Kenny continued. "But remember, God can use even the most broken vessels to bring others to Him. You have a gift, sister, a calling to be a soul winner. Don't be afraid to use it."

I nodded, feeling a sense of peace wash over me. Brother Kenny was right. I had been given a gift, a calling to share the love of Christ with others. And I knew that I couldn't let fear or doubt hold me back any longer.

As we stood on the bridge, the sky darkening around us, I made a silent vow to myself. I would be a soul winner, a messenger of God's love and grace. I would share the gospel with everyone I met, no matter how difficult or uncomfortable it might be.

And as I looked out at the river below, the lights of the city twinkling in the distance, I knew that God was with me, guiding me every step of the way. And with Brother Kenny by my side, I was ready to take on whatever challenges lay ahead.

The ~A~ bridge became a symbol of my journey, a place where I had found hope and strength in the midst of my struggles. And as I walked away with Brother Kenny, ready to face whatever the future held, I knew that I was exactly where I was meant to be—in the arms of God, ready to share His love with the world.

Love you all,
Prophet Brandon L. Davis
soonerthanrightnow@yahoo.com
bricklettermedia@gmail.com

10

BONUS

<u>Prophet Brandon L</u>
<u>Homework</u>

1. God is one; not only is there no other, but He is alone in being able to meet the deepest needs and longings of our hearts. God alone is worthy of our worship and devotion (Deuteronomy 6:4).

2. God is righteous, meaning that God cannot and will not pass over wrongdoing. It is because of God's righteousness and justice that, in order for our sins to be forgiven, Jesus had to experience God's wrath when our sins were placed upon Him (Exodus 9:27; Matthew 27:45-46; Romans 3:21-26).

3. God is sovereign, meaning He is supreme. All of His creation put together cannot thwart His purposes (Psalm 93:1; 95:3; Jeremiah 23:20).

4. God is spirit, meaning He is invisible (John 1:18; 4:24). God is a Trinity. He is three in one, the same in substance, equal in power and glory.

5. God is truth, He will remain incorruptible and cannot lie (Psalm 117:2; 1 Samuel 15:29).

6. God is holy, separated from all moral defilement and hostile toward it. God sees all evil, and it angers Him. God is referred to as a consuming fire (Isaiah 6:3; Habakkuk 1:13; Exodus 3:2, 4-5; Hebrews 12:29). God is gracious, and His grace includes His goodness, kindness, mercy, and love if it were not for.

7. God's grace and His holiness would exclude us from His presence. Thankfully, this is not the case, for He desires to know each of us personally (Exodus 34:6; Psalm 31:19; 1 Peter 1:3; John 3:16, 17:3).

He Decided to Die!
<u>INTRO</u>

It was now about the sixth hour, and there was darkness over the whole land until the ninth hour, while the sun's light failed, and the curtain of the temple was torn in two. Then Jesus, crying with a loud voice, said, "Father, into thy hands I commit my spirit!" And having said this, he breathed his last. Now, when the centurion saw what had taken place, he praised God and said, "Certainly, this man was innocent!" And all the multitudes who assembled to see the sight, when they saw what had taken place, returned home beating their breasts. And all his acquaintances and the women who had followed him from Galilee stood at a distance and saw these things.

(Luke 23:44-49)

To recap

<u>Three utterances concerned Man:</u>

1. to one he gave the promise to be with him in paradise
2. to another, he confided his mother
3. to the spectators, he mentions his thirst

<u>Three utterances concerned God</u>

1. to the Father, He prayed for forgiveness of those who knew not what they did
2. to God, he utters a complaint of being forsaken
3. and now to His Father, He declares it is finished and commits His Spirit

As we close out this session tonight, I want to submit three things to you today as we survey the cross.

<u>Prophetic on the Cross</u>

- In connection with each of the cross utterances by our Saviour, a prophecy was fulfilled.
- First, He cried Father, forgive them, which was fulfilled in Isaiah 53:12 as he made intercession for the transgressors.
- Second, He promised the thief Today You'll be with me in paradise, which fulfilled the angel's words to Joseph (Mt. 1:21) ..he shall save the people from their sins.
- Third, the cry to his mother was a fulfillment of Simeon, who said in Luke 2:35, A sword shall pierce thy soul.

- His complaint to God in the 4th utterance is identical to the one in Psa. 22:1
- Then the psalmist declared in Ps. 69:21, I thirst.

Yes, JESUS came to fulfill all things, and we can now see his prophetic work on the cross.

And so Jesus here, with his last uttering with a **loud voice,** "Father into thy hands I commend my spirit," Suggests a turnaround. There was a shift on the cross. Somebody say SHIFT! He was no longer forsaken and rejected. With his fully God yet fully human self, he went from nothing to something, from no words and darkness over the land to muster up with a loud voice and cry out to His Father. While he hung on the cross seven times, his lips moved in speech. The number 7 means completion perfection. He had completed the work given to him. His work was to destroy the works of the devil and to seek and save that which was lost. Yes, this was It; things were finished and now accomplished. He was about to do it! Breathe his last breath. See, everything that happened up until now was practice—running for his life while a child, being hidden away until due time, suffering and rejection before the cross and on the cross. It was practice. Now was the fullness of time come. The time of all things being complete was at hand. On the sixth day of creation, God said it was good and brought his work of creation to completion. And here, at the 7th utterance, Christ is at a place of rest in the Father's hands.

See, he had to die. There was no other way to buy back our freedom, for he is our redeemer (psm 69:18) . For without the shedding of blood, there is no remission (Hebrews 10:18) . He was wounded for our transgression and bruised for our iniquities by his stripes we are healed. He had to die! Otherwise, he would not have been our redeemer; he would not have been our waymaker. No! If Jesus had not died and been bruised, we could not claim our healing. John 12:27 says that for this cause, I came to die. Yes -- There was no other way. So, he made a conscious decision to lay down his life. **HE DECIDED TO DIE.** AND SO HIS DEATH ON THE CROSS WAS VOLUNTARY

<u>Voluntary on the Cross</u>

His work on the cross was prophetic because it fulfilled what had been said in the scriptures, but it was also voluntary (as He had said, "No man takes my life, but I lay it down").

I like how the gospel writers give us a complete picture of the cross. If you've read all the accounts in the

Synoptics and also John's Gospel, you get a vivid picture of the scene.

For example:

- **Luke 23:** "...and having said this, He gave up the ghost."
- **Mark 15:37:** "And Jesus cried with a loud voice and gave up the ghost."

But Matthew and Johns Gospel:

- **Matthew 27:50** says: "Jesus when He had cried again, yielded up the ghost."
- **John 19:30** reads: "...and He bowed His head and gave up the ghost."

In **Luke and Mark**, there is a single word used in Greek or Hebrew for the phrase "gave up," and it translates to mean [breathe out or expire].

The Gospels of **Matthew and John,** however, use unique phrasing. These are the only two references in the Bible that translate into a Greek phrase of two words, meaning *give over* or *deliver up*.

Why is this important? Keywords in *Luke and Mark* **breathed out or expired.** This tells says that he did die! The gospels of *Matthew and John,* however, show us **How** He died. It is important to note because it paints a complete picture of his work on the cross. It's not just enough to know that he died but that it was a Voluntary Death – (he gave it over, or you can say he delivered it up)<u>. **He decided to die.** </u>He made the ultimate sacrifice. He could have chosen another cup; He could have avoided capture, and he could have called a legion of angels. But no! He was led away as a lamb for the slaughter. He submitted! He came down 42 generations, even to the death of the cross. He delivered himself into the hands of sinners and delivered His spirit up to the Hands of a capable God. Yes, he Died. He didn't swoon or faint, as critiques would report. No! He died! **He breathed his last breath** on that cross (as Luke and Mark would say), But He died (thoughtfully, voluntarily, and purposefully) as Matthew and John would say. He – **DECIDED – to DIE!!!** He knew Greater was coming, After the suffering, after the rejection...He said, "Father, I commend my spirit into your hands. He could submit himself confidently into those *anthropomorphic* hands because he had already seen it. He was with God as he set the end from the beginning and still decided to die........ in powerful, omnipotent hands. And that same God secured a place for us. So it was a prophetic work, a voluntary work and an

<u>Eternal work on the Cross</u>

He had us in mind from the beginning. He made a way for us (humanity) to escape from the beginning. I submit to you today that the Father in Heaven has secured our future. And if you've placed yourself in the Father's hands, you too can be secure in your eternal future.

Your future can be secured better than Fort Knox. You can be in hands better than Allstate. For more than 12 hours, Christ had been in the hands of men, but here, at the end—He is in the hands of His Father. That lets us know that as the Father loved Christ, so does He love His children. I submit to you today that whether or not one has received Jesus does not change the fact that "For God so loved the world that He gave His only begotten Son, that whosoever believes in Him shall have everlasting, eternal life!" But it also says, "As many as received Him... Jesus would become the sons and daughters of God."

IS THAT YOU?? DO YOU HAVE A RIGHT TO CALL HIM FATHER... ABBA FATHER, DADDY... LORD...?

You may say, "I'm not against Him," but if you haven't made a decision for Him—the Christ—if you have not received the word of the cross, woe unto you. We, too, should desire to land in God's hands rather than in another's hands. **The Bible** says it is a **dreadful thing** to fall into the hands of a living God. **But it also says: don't be afraid** of those who kill the body but cannot kill the soul. Rather, be afraid of the One who can destroy both body and soul in Hell. **When your name is called, and you round the corner to make it home...he will say to you in the words of that eternal Umpire SAFE! SAFE! SAFE!**

So you can confidently say, as we were taught of old:

"Now I lay me down to sleep,

I pray to the Lord for my soul to keep.

If I should die before I wake,

I pray to the Lord for my soul to take."

Galatians 2:20